A Gesture of Words

To Trudy —
In admiration —
and in appreciation,
Yours in Poetry.

John

A Gesture of Words

Poetry Forms and Formulas

John F. Foster

CHB Media
Publisher

ISBN 978-1-5136-1496-0
LIBRARY OF CONGRESS CONTROL NUMBER: 2016952726

CHB MEDIA, PUBLISHER

(386) 690-9295
chbmedia@gmail.com
www.chbmediaonline.com

First Edition
Printed in the USA

Contents

The Poetry

Acknowledgements

Great thanks to my daughter, Elizabeth, who has served as my tech guru over the years. She is responsible for realizing my conception for the cover of this volume and for helping to edit its manuscript. I am grateful as well to my loving wife, Lorraine, for her constant support of all my poetic efforts. I am blessed to have them both in my life.

I am indebted to my very knowledgeable publisher, Gary Broughman, generous with his time and professional in every way.

Additional thanks to my dear friend and fellow poet, Yvonne Ponsor, who has graciously written a foreword to this collection.

A further "gesture of words" to my friends Peter Meinke, Poet Laureate of Florida, Al Rocheleau, extraordinary teacher and poet, and Joe Cavanaugh, former President of the Florida State Poets Association, 2012 – 2016. Their support of my work is hugely appreciated.

Lastly, for their interest in my poetics, a word of appreciation to poet friends in Florida: members of the Florida State Poets Association (FSPA), the New River Poets chapter of the FSPA, and especially my friend Janet Watson, the Selby Poets of Sarasota and the amazing group of Southshore Poets in the Sun City Center area.

— John F. Foster

"I am not a teacher, but an awakener."

— Robert Frost, American poet
1874 - 1963

Other Publications by John F. Foster

❖ *Discovery! A Wordcrafter's Journey*, published by Outskirts Press, 2009.

A unique blend of wit, wisdom and wordplay, this collection offers themes ranging from inspirational and philosophical to tongue-in-cheek commentary on the human condition. Special features of Foster's books are his personal comments for each poem and his "Poetry Reference Pages" which explain the variety of forms presented.

❖ *Chuckles—Verses to a-Muse*, published by XLibris, 2010.

A collection of humorous poetry in a variety forms ranging from the limerick to the Higgledy-Piggledy, from the McWhirtle to the Tetractys. Reference pages explain each form used in the volume which also contains a "Poet's comment" for each poem.

❖ *Where There's A Quill*, published by XLibris, 2011.

A thorough examination of 20 poetic forms with ample illustrations of each. In free verse, formal verse and light verse the poet has infused this volume with his trademark humor and insight, offering a personal commentary on each page and a glossary explaining each poetic form.

Preface

The purpose of this book is to acquaint the reader with a wide variety of poetic forms. My hope is that in doing so the reader will want to experiment with these different forms and create something that fulfills its own unique identity—that sheds to some degree the conventional garb of modern verse. By no means is this an exhaustive study. The 33 examples explained and illustrated in this collection are but a fraction of the many kinds of fixed verse found among the cultures of our world.

I developed a passion for poetry in 2008 when, at age 75, I discovered a web site with links to a cornucopia of poetic information. With such access at my fingertips, I came to appreciate the enormous variety of verse forms available to the poet. Some of the fixed forms in this book will be familiar to the reader, while others (the Burmese Ya-Du and Than Bauk, for example) are virtually unknown in the western world. All have specific structural requirements. Because of a predilection for wordsmithing, my passion for such special forms continues undiminished. As if working a crossword puzzle, I find myself delighted by the challenge of fitting words into a poetic grid.

Some free verse advocates will scoff at the idea of being fettered by requirements of line repetition, meter, rhyme and syllable count. I, on the other hand, take pleasure in attempting to produce a poem which satisfies such requirements in a way that can appear and sound unforced. I hasten to add, however, that I am not disenchanted with free verse (there are examples here to balance out the fixities) which has its own set of challenges[1]. In addition to the free verse in this collection, I offer a number of rhymed and metered poems which fall under no category and are not labeled as to type.

As in all my books, I include a "Poet's comment" below each poem, a kind of Post Scriptum for the reader. In this particular volume there is an index at the back which will direct you to the page where each poetry form is introduced.

Finally, I hope that you, the reader, will find this volume both instructive and entertaining. If these pages can inspire you to take on the challenge[2] of some of these forms, then my purpose with this book will have been fulfilled.

— John F. Foster

[1] Although free verse requires no meter, rhyme, spacing or other poetic techniques, a poet can still use them to create sound patterns and a sense of structure and flow. It is, in fact, the internal pattern of sounds, the rich and precise vocabulary and the effect of associations which can give free verse its beauty and power.

[2] A word to those ready for the challenge: the following forms lend themselves more to light, whimsical themes rather than to more somber subjects: Clerihew, Minute Poem, Tetractys, Higgledy Piggledy, Limerick, McWhirtle and Diminished Pentaverse.

Foreword

John Foster is a poet for all reasons.

His love of language and his creative drive combine with his ability to inspire people to find and to nurture—give voice and substance to—their poetic selves.

John never met a poet he didn't like. That's not to say he's not discriminating. On the contrary, he works diligently to find what's good in each piece—the hope, the vision or the personality that inspired it. In a workshop atmosphere of congeniality and devotion, where he shares poetic experience with others seeking to find a voice, his comments are helpful and specific.

He defines and illuminates the structure and style of poetic expression, from sonnet to haiku and beyond. This book on forms is a necessary tool to prod the imagination. New ways to combine rhyme and rhythm can work to let the poet express feeling and mood.

John is a man of generous spirit and useful intellect. His good humor, his *joie de vivre*, are alive in his writing. He likes unusual words—interrobang, somniloquent, paraprosdokian— and how they feel in the mouth. He encourages people to experiment. Recently, he got me so hooked on haiku that I could only think in 5 – 7 – 5 syllable thoughts! He continues to astonish people by saying, "Look at that, you have written a perfect tetrameter poem! What a gem!" And everybody feels good.

But best of all, he writes poetry. Good poetry! His output ranges from laugh-out-loud funny to the sensitive and poignant, from the arcane to the obvious. He writes with intuition and humility . His talent is imaginative and visionary. His depth and reach are demonstrated in the poetry collected here—with lots of wit, lots of joy, and a tear or two.

This is your chance to hear the voice of a true poet.

Yvonne Ponsor, B.A., M.A., HL.D
Publications: *Gawain and the Green Night, 1989,*
The Death of a Waterman, 2013.

A Gesture Of Words

A poem may be thought of as a gift,
a gesture of words in tissued layers wrapped,
its crucial message placed beneath the folds,
its secret *raison d´être* yet untapped.

A poem may present itself unwrapped,
but framed in language rich, and yet transparent,
its natural state devoid of bows and ribbon;
its simple elegance becomes apparent.

As words of welcome or at times good-byes,
or sometimes, too, to mark a moment dire.
A proffered thought of caring for a loved one,
a noble verse intended to inspire.

A bedtime gift recited in the nurs'ry
in all its wondrous fantasy and rhyme,
a verbal present given at a birthday
to pause and mark the tread of Father Time.

These worded gifts a treasure to discover
and when poetic savoring is done,
the reader and the list'ner can delight in
poetry's place forever in the sun.

Poets comment: First Place winner in a 2015 contest for poetry
sponsored by the National Federation of State Poetry Societies.
The contest called for poetry with the theme of the NFSPS
national convention: *Discover the Treasure—Poetry's Place in the
Sun*.

Wing

Into tindered hills he climbs
through lifeless char and blister
and smoldering rock.

Fire-rigged and vigilant for damage done,
he probes the smoking earth,
charting an inferno.

Eyes burning and ashen-faced,
he discovers a bird sitting petrified in firedust
at the foot of a barren pine.

A careful nudge and three tiny chicks scurry back
under their dead mother's wing.

Disaster impending, a loving mother
had carried her offspring to the base of a tree
and gathered them under her wing,

instinctively knowing smoke would rise.

From a sudden sob, a single teardrop
softly splashes into the ash
of a small, scorched body.

A body once warm with life,
and maternal,
and steadfast.

Poet's comment: This poem is based on an account reported in the aftermath of the Great Yellowstone Fire of 1977. Second place award to poems about birds, sponsored by the Christian poetry journal *Time For Singing*.

John Foster

Dawning

What triggered an ancestral grunt,
poetic sentiment beside a prehistoric flame,
or caused a first impression to be made upon Euphrates mud,
or scrawled across a cavern wall?

Perhaps a latent pulsing in some hominid
grew warm inside a stone age heart,
emerging first a groping gutturals
tramsmuted later into oral modes ...
then ideography (a charcoal one?)
in passion scratched upon a flat banana leaf
to be beheld and then beloved
as the phenomenon of poetry.

Poet's Comment: Imagining the origins of our craft. My first
effort at free verse (which I had shunned for years), this
poem was selected to be offered as a bookmark to registrants
at the 2010 convention of the Florida State Poets Associa-
tion.

FLIN Poem

A verse which builds on the first line of a well-known poem, preserving the meter and/or rhyme scheme of the original.

This poem is based on James W. Foley's Drop A Pebble In The Water.

FLIN derives its name from the words First LINe.

John Foster

Flare Out

Drop a pebble in the water, just a splash and it is gone....

Momentary bloom created on a pastel surface, drawn.

Like a plant that saves its glory for a final burst of bloom,

or a supernova story—incandescent light, then gloom.

For a brief ecstatic moment, insects mate and then may die.

Wondering: At death, does man's creative force intensify?

Poet's comment: Speculating about my burst of poetic creativity from age 75 to 83.

Museum Piece

Its unique façade smoothed by the ages,
dark granite resplendent with illumination,
this artifact posing in quiet splendor
spans twenty centuries.

Most visited of all museum pieces in Britain,
paling even the Crown Jewels,
one simple fragment of antiquity
has become a symbol of its own crowning achievement.

Upon its flank a royal decree
marking the first anniversary of
a 13-year-old
pharaoh.

That this decree was
carved in Greek,
chiseled in Demotic and
hammered in hieroglyph
has made all the difference.

The Rosetta Stone.

Key to the mysteries of ancient Egypt.
Connector of civilizations.
Bridge of enlightenment.

Poet's comment: A tribute not only to the artifact, but to the Frenchman Jean-François Champollion who, in 1822, deciphered the Egyptian hieroglyphs.

John Foster

In Another Life

In another life, I'd dare
To show the enemy I care.

In another life, I'd try
To tell the painful truth, not lie.

In another life, I'd fight
Against the odds, if that were right.

In another life I'd be
A stronger, truer, better me.

In another life, I'd know
Achieving this might not be so.

Poet's comment: The result of a challenge by the New River
Poets (a chapter of the Florida State Poets Association) to write a
poem using the element of repetition.

Pleiades

A 7-line poem, unrhymed, with a single word title.
The first letter of the title must be used to begin each
line. No other requirements. The Pleiades were the
7 daughters of Atlas who, in Greek mythology, were
turned into a group of stars making up what is now the
constellation of the same name. A more challenging
form of the Pleiades requires six syllables per line.

John Foster

Waterfall

Winter brook meanders,
Winds crystalline o'er slopes
Where, with melted snow, it
Widens, swollen, dashing
With purpose now across
Worn boulders, rushing down
Wildly, splashing, crashing!

Poet's comment: Attempting to evoke the increasing rush of water.

Trellis
(Pleiades)

Trailing honeysuckle
Tumbles freely over
Twisting vines of jasmine.
Tethered pink clematis
Thread through morning glories,
Tantalizing nostrils
Together as they bloom.

Poet's comment: Reminding me of a visit to a factory in Grasse, capital of France's perfume industry.

John Foster

Dream House

Like dessert at the end of a meal,
the Saturday matinee waited temptingly
while we salivated during the week.

Our neighborhood theater, its marquee
a cake of layered enticements,
stood in art-deco'd splendor
along Main Street.

Our dream house.

At the portal, posters signaled coming attractions,
their candy-wrapper colors beckoning.
We could just taste it.

In those days,
getting there was at least a quarter of the fun!

And indeed, it was a quarter
to earn our way in—
sitting for baby brother,
the relentless lawn,
those dinner dishes.

Five nickels of pure escape
into MovieTone News, Travelogs,
Tom Mix, Tom and Jerry and
Wow! The double feature.

More than a mini film festival,
our matinee was, to us,
a delicious weekend confection.

Poet's comment: Nourishing nostalgia.

A Gesture of Words

Clogyrnach

A quantitative syllabic stanza of Welsh origin. Six lines combining one couplet of eight syllables, one couplet of five syllables and the final two lines of three syllables. Rhyming is aabbba.

John Foster

U.S. Open Playoff

Golf history in the making
was Mediate's for the taking.
Tiger won instead
in a head-to-head,
on pain med.
He's aching!

Poet's comment: Recalling Tiger Wood's dramatic victory in 2008
while playing with a painful knee condition.

Ode To My Home Town

I'm sorry to disturb ya by returning to suburbia,
like a cat upon your township I have pounced

to find the very essence of my awkward adolescence,
so here I am arriving unannounced.

My Muse perceives me clinging to your role in my upbringing,
for example those parades for well-known causes.

With my Cub Scout troop so hep to parading out of step
and with all our dads dressed up as Santa Clauses.

Country fairs for all the town folk and the legendary town joke,
throwing sponges at our mayor feigning drunk.

He would teeter, then he'd totter balanced o'er a tank of water.
When we hit him it was truly a "slam dunk"!

At our picnic by the water, Sally Ann, my neighbors' daughter,
(over whom I gawked and panted and I drooled),

brought a cake for me to taste, topped with fresh wallpaper paste,
and I knew that I'd been truly "April Fooled."

Once our movie house was victim—oh, the owner how we tricked him,
sneaking inside for a week end matinee.

"Hey, you kids!" we heard him holler, as he grabbed us by the collar.
We knew then that there'd be holy hell to pay.

While it isn't total bliss to reflect and reminisce,
I am glad I've had a chance to resurrect,

without much thought to etiquette, my hometown in Connecticut
while stressing the *first* part that spells C-O-N-N-E-C-T.

John Foster

Sincerely,
John F. Foster

Poet's comment: Composed in response to a challenge by the New River Poets chapter of the Florida State Poets Association to write a poem addressed to one's home town, in this case Darien, Connecticut. Ah, those were the days!

Double Dactyl

Otherwise known as a "Higgledy Piggledy," the verse is almost always humorous. It consists of two four-line stanzas in dactyl meter (dah-dit-dit, as in elephant, camouflage, editor, peek-a-boo). The first line is always rhyming nonsense (though here you may note an obvious reason for concocting the first line of these poems). Line two introduces the subject of the poem, often a person's name. Additionally, there must be a single double dactyl word in the second stanza. Finally the last word of each stanza must rhyme.

John Foster

Staking A Claim

Biggery Diggery
Anthony Wickersham
boasts I'm in love at age
ninety, you see.

She's a professor of
paleontology;
I know she'll love an old
fossil like me!

Poet's comment: One of my favorite fixed forms (though not one
of the easiest to write!). Randomly, the word "paleontology"
crossed my mind one day. When I realized it was a double dactyl
word, I decided to build a Higgledy Piggledy around it.

Spotcha! Gotcha!
(Higgledy Piggledy)

Teachery Featury
Portia Lee Paranoid
had sev'ral eyes in the
back of her head,

thereby reducing the
classroom shenanigans.
"Omnidirectional
Radar," she said.

Poet's comment: I had a third grade teacher (partially paranoid—
see line 2) who always seemed to know what was going on while
facing the blackboard.   Sound familiar?

John Foster

Bivalve
(double dactyl)

Hithery-Dithery
Dee Licious Cockleshell
fluttered her valves to an-
nounce she was "bi."

All the he-shells being
heterosexual,
didn't know whether to
give her a try.

Poet's comment: you may wonder about line 3. I was happy to discover that double-dactyls allow for hyphenation in order to conform to metric requirements. Once again I'm doing something more with the nonsense phrase of line 1.

In A Basement
(Higgledy Piggledy)

OH-nonny, NO-nonny,
Nicholas Goalsworthy
promised again to
renounce alcohol;

characteristically
incomprehensible,
muttering epithets,
cursing a wall.

Poet's comment: Going against convention with this serious
theme. The duality of the title and the first line provide hints
of what is to follow. For good measure, I have filled the second
stanza with two double dactyl words.

John Foster

Bees' Buzz

It behooves us to examine
How our honey bees behave.
Crisis of the honey famine.
Apiary business save?

Disappearance enigmatic—
Are they dead or still alive?
Nature's order gone erratic
In behavior of beehive.

Poet's comment: The mystery remains.

McWhirtle

A light verse similar to the double dactyl (higgledy-piggledy) in structure and rhyme. It was invented in 1989 by American poet Bruce Newling. The McWhirtle adds an extra unstressed syllable at the beginning of each stanza. Syllables may move from the end of one line to the beginning of the next for readability. Dactyl meter. Usually humorous.

Up And Away!

Deep down in the cannon was
Clarence the Cannonball,
ready to dazzle the crowd
with his grit.

Kaboom! Out the barrel, he
overshot safety net,
finding his dream to become
A "smash hit"!

Poet's comment: Icarus the Second. Third HM in contest for a humorous poem written in formal verse, sponsored by the Florida State Poets Association.

Fast Colors

The maroon and grey ribbon
that once tied us together
has unraveled into
a lengthy strip of years.

But we have held fast
to those colors and
though the ribbon has laid down
different paths for us, its colors
have not faded over time.

Our Loomis Chaffee ribbon
decorates us all
with pride of school,
knowledge, character.

And at reunion,
it binds us again together,
as we were ...
students, classmates, friends.

Poet's comment: Composed for my 60th class reunion at the Loomis Chaffee School. In my absence it was read at our class dinner. Later I made it into a bookmark which I distributed personally to returning alumni at our 65th reunion.

John Foster

Sharing

Exploring a country road, I stop to view
a nursery beside a church.
Caregivers both, I decide,
for they stand together in their nurturing.
Shrubs and souls. Each with its mission
to beautify.

And as I draw closer to their doors,
I smile at the signposts which
(as if to twin themselves again)
spell out:

SOD AVAILABLE   **GOD AVAILABLE**

Poet's comment: A local nursery for years has advertised with
a "Sod Available" sign. The rest is "what if......?" 2nd HM for
religious poetry in a contest sponsored by Poets & Patrons, Inc.,
2014

Shakespearean Sonnet

A 14-line lyric poem consisting of 3 quatrains (4-line stanzas) and a concluding couplet (2 rhyming lines). It was not invented by Shakespeare, but named for him because he was its most famous practitioner.
Its lines by tradition are written in iambic pentameter.
Its rhyme scheme is abab, cdcd, efef, gg.

John Foster

Bed Side

His fingers slide across the vacant sheet
to smooth away the wrinkles lying there,
where once her perfumed presence warmed his sleep,
his searching palms embracing only air.

He reaches for her pillow just as if
the hug of it might somehow ease his pain,
and breathes her very essence in a sniff
that turns into a sniffle sobbed in vain.

He cannot bring himself to make the bed,
nor draw the coverlet up over all,
so sweeps the sheet with deep caress instead
and weeps afresh to contemplate the pall.

For ever-endless nights beside her side,
he wonders why his young bride could have died.

Poet's comment: Second place winner of a poem for sonnets
sponsored by *Harp Strings Poetry Journal.*

Wind Chimes
(Shakespearean sonnet)

On days with windows open to the sky,
My mother would, with faintest trace of smile,
Step out into the warmth of our lanai,
Then pause and stare and listen for a while.

And presently she'd reach up to unclasp
The iridescent crystals swaying there.
The tantalizing tinkle in her grasp,
She'd bring the music in for us to share.

Once gently placed above the open bay,
Its colors dancing on the curtains' wings,
Our instrument would then begin to play
Its grace notes like a fairy choir sings.

So often when I'm faced with troubled times,
I bring to mind our ritual of the chimes.

Poet's comment: Warm memories. Third place winner in a
contest for formal verse sponsored by the FSPA, 2013.

John Foster

Choices
(Shakespearean sonnet)

So little do we have control of fate,
We might, in moments of distress, reflect
Upon a sense of helplessness innate,
Succumbing to a tide of self-neglect.

In truth, we have no choice about our birth,
Its circumstance in fate's uncertain hand.
We cannot dictate when upon the earth
We might start life, and in what native land.

No choice of parents likewise is our lot,
Nor any say in death's unknowing plan,
The when and where of which we oft cannot
Predict. What then, the destiny of man?

Who claims this realm of choicelessness deprives?
We can and must choose how we live our lives.

Poet's comment: I came across the word "choicelessness" while reading a magazine in my dentist's office. It served to inspire this poem.

Flying The Web
(Shakespearean sonnet)

I wing into this world of cyberspace
And soar expectantly along the waves
Of poetry from some exotic place.
A thirsty sommelier of sorts who craves

A chance to savor lines from Ireland,
Or posted from the Southern Hemisphere
In some New Zealand writer's clever hand.
The poets of South Africa give ear

To poems I have offered on our site,
And I, in turn, give feedback for the words
That my poetic pen pals choose to write,
With lines that fly the globe as free as birds.

What Verne envisioned eighty days would take,
Such travels in an instant can I make.

Poet's comment: This poem was inspired by the web sites World
of Poets and Poets for Integrity which have led me to polish my
writing skills and to create friendships with poets far and near.
This sonnet earned a Third Honorable Mention in a nationwide
contest sponsored by the Florida State Poets Association

John Foster

A Light Touch
(Shakespearean sonnet)

She chooses from her sexy lingerie
A filmy, lacy number just for him.
She slips it on, the essence of risqué,
And slides into their bed; the lights grow dim.

Her husband's hands explore beneath the sheets,
His palms descending with increasing verve.
She now begins to shiver as she greets
His glancing touch, exciting every nerve.

The softest moan beseeches from her lips
as searching fingers further down then drop
And brush along her tantalizing hips....
He stops. She pleads *"Oh, honey, please don't stop!*

Hey, why'd you quit?", her voice a puzzled note.
His calm reply: *"I found it ... the remote."*

Poet's comment: Giving poetic voice to an old joke. 1st HM in the
Randall Cadman Memorial Award contest for formal verse, 2015.

Petrarchan Sonnet

The poet Petrarch developed this form of the Italian
sonnet which, written in iambic pentameter, consists
of two parts, an octave (eight lines) and a sestet (six
lines). The octave typically contains a rhyme scheme
of abbaabba and traditionally introduces a problem,
reflects on reality, or expresses a desire. It often
presents a situation that causes doubt or conflict within
the speaker. The beginning of the sestet is known as the
"volta" and introduces a pronounced change in tone. The
sestet is more flexible in its rhyming; a popular scheme
is cdecde. The sestet's purpose is to make a comment on
the problem or apply a solution to it.

John Foster

Fine Dining

He entered first, three steps ahead of her,
Without a thought of holding out the door,
As if he were intending to ignore
Her token presence, knowing she'd defer.
Demanding service by the restauranteur,
He took his seat, ignoring her once more.
Like mannequins they sat, without rapport.
A wordless couple, disengaged they were.
Now, we may wonder why the vacant eyes,
The rote and flatly rude behavior seen,
And speculate about this loveless pair.
A dark betrayal of their nuptial ties?
Two tired souls, their lives a dull routine?
Whatever be the answer, would they care?

Poet's comment: Inspired (and disconcerted) by a couple's behavior in a local restaurant.

Imprint

He staggered imperceptibly
and leaned against his cane,
the white-haired man ahead of me
in line; he winced in pain.

I asked if he would like to sit;
I'd hold on to his spot
until the nurse with vaccine kit
was ready with his shot.

He said at once: "No thanks, my friend.
I'll keep my place in line.
You see, I've learned not to depend
on others ... I'll be fine."

Determination, courage, too,
were etched upon his face.
He winced again with pain anew,
but firmly held his place.

And much to my amazement, he
then brightened with a smile,
and said: "You know, I plan to be
around for quite a while!"

This man's a real survivor type,
it surely seemed to me.
Not one complaint, nor any gripe.
A great example, he.

We then continued to converse
until he took his leave.
Still smiling, he approached the nurse
and now rolled up his sleeve.

John Foster

What followed left an imprint on
my mind and heart: I stared
at numbers tattooed there, upon
the forearm he had bared.

I knew at once what kind of man
had come into my life.
Imagine hardships (no one can)
in overcoming strife?

Poet's comment: Let us never forget....

Ekphrasis

The practice of using words to comment on a piece
of visual art, i.e. a novel about a film, a poem about a
painting, photograph, etc. Ekphrasic poetry is the poet's
descriptive response to the direct stimulus of a piece of
art with the poet's experience in the moment.

State Seal of Florida
(ekphrasis)

Native beauty paints the land,
hibiscus blossoms fall.
Sabal and palmetto stand
so proudly over all.

Steamboat sails before the sun,
rays reaching for the sky.
Industry has just begun,
the wheel would signify.

Like a spare but pithy verse,
the image of its seal
conveys the essence, rightly terse,
of Florida's appeal.

Poet's comment: Inspired by the symbolism of Florida's
state seal (see page opposite).

(see page opposite)

Brown Pelican

Such a feat of engineering,
proudly posing here.

Our attention commandeering
with that look severe.

And no wonder he's a proud one;
attributes unique.

He's a more than well-endowed one
with that scooper beak.

Only member of his species
diving vertically.

Air sacs keep him in one piece; he's
built to pierce the sea.

Eyes as sharp as any eagle's
often locate prey

far beyond the scope of seagulls
over Tampa Bay.

Poet's comment: My past seems connected with this remarkable
creature. The pelican is the mascot of my high school. I was
associated for many years with the Pelican Players, a local
community theater.

A View of The Cosmos

Peering beyond an arcing star-sequined sky,
Medieval man marvels.
Seeking paradise without leaving earth,
He has found his grail,
The locus where earth touches an opaque firmament.

Beyond the mysterious gateway,
A Jules Verne realm of cosmic machinery:
Circling clouds, fires, suns, cogs, and whirling wheels,
So removed, yet now accessible
From flat and fertile earth.

Kneeling, he lifts his hand
As if to hail his Maker,
The tinkering mechanic.

An inscription below marks
The terrestrial "cities" and celestial "spheres"
In cosmographic union.

Poet's comment: Based on the Flammarion Engraving (opposite page), so named because its first documented appearance is in Camille Flammarion's 1888 book, *L'atmosphère Météorologie Populaire*. The engraving is a woodcut by an unknown artist.

Le Penseur
(ekphrasis)

He sits in sinewed bronze, his toes contracted,
a torsioning of torso, right fist impacted
against the jaw, his mood a brood of thought,
this Florentine heroic nude by Rodin wrought.

The poet, Dante, in passioned struggle caught
imagining a Hell yet to be brought
to literary life, its scenes enacted
within his fertile mind, infernally redacted.

The statue's left hand open, not as taut,
as if the contemplator might have sought
to grasp elusive truth, and once extracted,
to reveal man's penance in a destiny protracted.

He sits upon that pediment of rock, attracted
by humanity's condition so abstracted
as to leave his deepest thinking fraught
with knots – and yet we know 'twas not for naught.

Poet's comment: On the facing page, Rodin's "Le Penseur" ("The Thinker"), graces the grounds of the Rodin Museum in Paris. These are speculations on what Dante might be contemplating. The back and forth of the assonance and consonance of the two rhymes is an attempt to suggest Dante's conflicted thinking.

When We Wore Wings

When we wore wings,
cherubs in a Christmas play,
we were transported into everlands
of Canaan and of Babylon whose names
were magically linked, it seemed, with Israel,
their cities cited as tradition told ...

That holy manger scene each year,
enacted with abiding sense of awe
in modest cloth or kingly robes Arabian,
brought forth a sense of love and miracles.

These lands were thus enchanted;
in our passion for His story,
we would have worn the Arab garb of kings
upon the stage (if we'd been older)
and adored the Jew.

And upon life's stage today?

Poet's comment: Enough said.

John Foster

Top of the Line

Astride a tempting hedge,
its feet splayed fan-like,
the egret stalks with satellite eyes,
beak arrowing its prey below.

Poised for a cobra-thrust
into a scurry of delicacies,
the sly predator
stands stealth-still,

while on a lower twig
the wily gecko, unaware,
plots to pounce upon
an unsuspecting ladybug

who, in turn, has spied
a ravenous aphid ...

Poet's comment: Nature's way.

Haiku

An unrhymed Japanese verse recording the essence
of a moment. The western version contains 3 lines
in a syllable arrangement of 5 – 7 – 5 (often fewer
syllables in modern haiku), and is customarily written
without punctuation or capitalization. Haiku poets
strive for depth, imagery, delicacy, subtlety within this
concise format. Often containing a seasonal reference,
traditional haiku name the subject in the first line and
elaborate on it in the second line. The final line may
represent a break in thought or offer an unexpected
conclusion.

John Foster

Beauty Spots

colorless puddles
become windows into blue
as clouds disappear

Poet's comment: I have elected to give my haiku a title, although
this practice is not the norm.

Thirst
(haiku)

sunbaked arroyo
parched pebbles
distant thunderclap

Poet's comment: Fewer syllables this time.

John Foster

Sylvan Symphony
(haiku)

faint rhythmic whirring
wings sing as softest wind chimes
wood nymphs in concert

Poet's comment: Close your eyes and listen.

Scarecrow

What pulled me to a stop?

Steel wool clouds
pulsing neon in the backlit distance,
or a narrow beam of sunlight
brushstroking the autumn foliage?

Or the tilted scarecrow flapping
a greeting from its field
of barren bristle? A shepherd
with no flock to tend.

Listing sideways in the gathering wind,
the weathered sentinel beckoned
as if to invite a visit.
Was it a supplication?

I stepped across empty scraggle
seeking evidence from long ago.
Flattened furrows, embedded perhaps
with composting greens? Stalks? Vines?

Nothing more than scrub and thorn
and desolate dust.
So why in this wasteland,
my ancient friend?

A sharp gust, as if in reply, coughed across the field
and heaved against the weak-rooted figure
knocking its wooden frame
to the ground.

John Foster

Rushing as though in rescue,
I crouched beside my beleaguered host
and stared at what lay beneath its torn-away shirt –
a painted inscription across its arms and chest:

"Future home of the cross — your Calvary Church".

Poet's comment: There is, in a vacant field on a nearby stretch of road, a sign containing the final line of this poem. Somewhat sadly, it has remained there for many years. Its place in that empty field represents the seed of this poem.

Legacy Lost

... and then I paused
and turned for one last look.

The family farm,
once a Winslow Homer painting
of proud permanence,
had caved.

Three generations.
I of the fourth would no longer till,
nor plant, nor harvest here,
nor die here.

Forebears had staked a claim—
worked it, stoned it,
owned it.

My claim, hollow
as the empty barn.

The Winslow Homer,
cracked and peeling,
unfit even for auction,
now chattled to a bank.

I glanced back at the great oak,
its wisps of moss floating in the wind
like clusters of hands waving
good-bye.

I wanted to turn back
the clock.

Poet's comment: Alas.

John Foster

Envisioning

Night's dewdrop cloud
caresses the still of a misty landscape.
Seeping through the haze,
dawn glistens green.

A grassy park. Children playing.
A boy and girl pause over
an arena of mushrooms
bursting, boasting being Nature's
"overnight sensation."

For her, a social circle has emerged,
sunbonneted, a klatch preening
into existence, gossiping
in their sueded splendor.

 For him, helmets huddled
in the wild, ragged formation
of fledgling football;
a clustered bluster poised perhaps
to poison an offensive move?

Mushrooming imaginations at play.
Poets in the making.

Poet's comment: My inspiration sprang from a neighbor's lawn.

Senryu — (pronounced sen-ree-yoo)

Unrhymed Japanese verse, similar to haiku.
Senryu contain three lines often arranged in a 5 – 7 – 5
syllable format. Modern senryu may be found with
fewer syllables. Like haiku, senryu are traditionally
written without punctuation or capitalization and offer
no title. Whereas haiku speak of nature, senryu concern
themselves with human nature and can, for example, be
emotional, playful, sarcastic, humorous.

John Foster

Grace

family dinner
father's voice breaks
empty high chair

Poet's comment: Sigh.

Burn The Candles
(senryu)

avoid saving best
for a special occasion
today is special

Poet's comment: Another slant on "carpe diem."

John Foster

Fortune Cookie
(senryu)

war not determine
who is right   it determine
in fact who is left

Poet's comment: Amen.

Short Story

Secret egret
eye spies.
Newt scoots.

Poet's comment: Not intended as a senryu. Rather, a lighthearted attempt to produce a rhyming saga. On a more serious note, I cannot help but think of Hemingway's famous six-word story, often labeled the shortest story ever written: "Baby shoes for sale. Never worn."

John Foster

Foreplay

She tilts her head back knowingly,
awaiting his caress,
and eyes his fingers glowingly,
desire to express.

She inches forward proffering
her nape for tender touch,
her body writhing, offering
the charms he loves so much.

His musky scent intoxicates;
she moans in ecstasy.
Her warmth upon him radiates
her physicality.

He blows a whisper in her hear
while tickling at her chin.
Her shiver at his voice so near
brings on a knowing grin.

He gently carries her to bed
and turns off hallway light.
He pats her on her feline head,
then bids his cat good night.

Poet's Comment: Oh, well ...

Abecedarian

A poem of 26 lines, each of which begins with a
successive letter of the alphabet.
Lines may consist of one or more words.

John Foster

Love Letter

A
Better
Chance,
Dear
Elizabeth.
Friendship
Gone
Haywire.
I
Just
Know
Letters
Might
Nudge
Our
Partnership,
Quench
Restless
Soul-searching,
Torturing us,
Virtually.
Wondering ...?
XXXX's
Your
Zachary

Poet's comment: When reading this poem, I think of how it must feel to the Japanese who read vertically.

Priorities

Early morning.
Violin strains sweep the crowded hall
of a DC metro station.

Bach is borne
on tunnel drafts, echoing deep
and hollow
for thousands.

Seventeen minutes – sixty-three cents.

Continuous display of sound;
no pause by the master
nor by commuters listening
for the next train.

Twenty-eight minutes – two dollars and two cents.

Tot looks back, his mother tugging.

Woman with violin case glances at musician,
then at her watch.

Cell-bent teens oblivious ...

Drunk flips coin
into hat.

Forty-five minutes – four dollars and
no sense.

Six Bachs.
Not even six bucks.

John Foster

Six pieces in search of an audience,
no matter the virtuoso
known in other halls,
the concert stages of the world,
as Joshua Bell.

Poet's comment: Based on an experiment conducted by the American Psychological Association in which Joshua Bell agreed to play classical music in a Washington D.C. subway station. Third place in contest "Honoring Cole Porter Award" sponsored by the Indiana State Federation of Poetry Clubs, 2015.

On The Mark

An exclamation point and question mark,
in combination rarely used or seen
for emphasis in wide-eyed wonder stark,
or else some literary in-between?

Its nomenclature's somewhat logical,
and yet the word brings on the taste of slang.
It sounds far less than pedagogical,
the idle and ignored "interrobang."

This wondrous word is quite legitimate
and found in dictionaries nationwide.
I wonder why we're not more intimate
with such a term so useful, yet untried.

Perhaps confined to themes rhetorical,
exclamatory questions posed to self,
or innuendoes metaphorical;
it lies forsaken on the writer's shelf.

But hark! Some wakening publicity!
A sly wisecracker cracked in wry harangue,
while understanding the duplicity
implicit in the term "interrobang":

"It's like the inquisition at a bar
a guy is put through by a hungry dame,
before at last determining how far
he'll go for her to play the bedding game!"

This play vernacular upon the "mark"
should not deter us from another game
of bringing light to words lain in the dark,
allowing them a modest claim to fame.

John Foster

Poet's comment: Inspired by an article in Gene Weingarten's humor column for the Washington Post. Being both enlightened and entertained by the article, I determined to enshrine this wondrous curiosity in a poem. I then decided to share it with Mr. Weingarten. To my delight he replied with a generous "thank you" note. Those sensitive to meter may have noticed the iambic pentameter throughout.

Nonet

A 9-line verse of decreasing syllable counts. The first line contains nine syllables, the second line eight syllables, and so on down to the final line of one syllable. Rhyming is optional.

Release

When the taut and teeming coil of day
has eased its fevered self into
the quiet cool of twilight's
pastel pool, then I may
be at last released
unbound, unwound,
unspiralled
into
sleep.

Poet's comment: First place award for a poem about relaxation
open to FSPA members attending their annual convention in
2013.

The Nonet
(nonet)

The poetic form of the nonet
Makes one count syllables, and yet,
Flows from one line to the next
While making sense of text,
Each line reducing
Syllabically,
Producing
A terse
Verse.

Poet's comment: My first effort at a nonet, having just
learned its requirements.

John Foster

Sunset
(nonet)

Fiery sun descends, shimmering,
until sea gives birth to twin orbs
mirrored on the horizon.
And now with naked eye,
we stare in wonder
as blood-orange
slips away
and is
gone.

Poet's comment: Often taken for granted, this
phenomenon, when viewed for its own sake,
can be mesmerizing.

Wicked Plants

The hemlock's known for poisonous qualities,
the oleander, too …
and sumac offers no frivolities;
a pox for me and you.

The snakeroot plant is most notorious
for toxin's secret kill.
The pink foxglove, while looking glorious,
can be more lethal, still.

The rhubarb leaf is rhubarbarious,
just like poinsettias' are;
the deadly nightshade grows nefarious
from here to Zanzibar.

But there's a plant in toxicology –
a caveat to heed,
ignored by us, without apology:
the famed tobacco weed.

Poet's comment: I sympathize with anyone who has attempted to quit smoking. It took me six years to do so, and then, only with the help of a hypnotist. For those curious about the metrics, this piece contains alternating iambic pentameter and trimeter.

John Foster

Rain Dance

Life is surely something more
than waiting for a storm
to pass our earthly dwelling's door;
to some it seems the norm.

That feeling may we disavow
in singing this refrain:
Knowing life is knowing how
to dance in all the rain.

Poet's comment: If Gene Kelly can do it, we can do it!

Word Palindrome

A two-line verse in which each line reads the same way forwards and backwards. Most people are familiar with the letter palindrome, for example "Madam, I'm Adam". I cannot find examples of this variation, but I doubt if it's original.

Still Life

Will humans detract? Humans will.
Still life is life, still.

Poet's comment: If you can find other examples, let me know at lojofoster@gmail.com.

Endless
(word palindrome)

Seeds become flowers become seeds.
Replication of nature of replication.

Poet's comment: I'm reminded of the phrase "Ashes to ashes, dust to dust."
— From the Anglican Church's Book of Common Prayer.

John Foster

Whale Song

When the winches squeak in weighty unison,
hauling nets that hug the ocean floor,
the trawler's baleful call seeps full into the sea,
as might seductive siren songs pervade the Rhine.

And presently, like lepidoptera,
behemoths of the deep are drawn
into that squealing echo 'neath the waves.
A pod of spontaneity.

Surface gaiety erupts off starboard bow
in concert with the strains of straining gears,
and cresting equally, applause bursts forth
in homage to a splashing symphony of sound.

Poet's comment: Inspired by a scene from a film in which I learned
how the sound of a trawler's winches can lure these great crea-
tures.

Triolet

A poetic form of French origin likely dating to the 13th century. It is a verse of eight lines featuring repetition and rhyme. The 1st, 4th and 7th lines are identical, as are the second and final lines. Thus, the initial and final couplets are identical as well. With a rhyme scheme of ABaAabAB, the triolet is traditionally written in iambic tetrameter. The earliest triolets were devotionals written by Patrick Carey, a 17th century Benedictine monk. British poet Robert Bridges reintroduced the triolet to the English language in the 19th century where it was further popularized by Thomas Hardy.

Christmas Eve

Where voices now rejoice in song
And echo through the night,
We join the festive "sing along"
Where voices now rejoice in song
With carols—it's where we belong;
A fellowship by candlelight
Where voices now rejoice in song
And echo through the night.

Poet's comment: I've always sensed the musicality of the triolet
with its repetition and rhyme. Hence the theme of this poem.

Summer Breezes
(triolet)

While summer breezes lullaby
My senses into sleep,
I breathe a long and languid sigh
While summer breezes lullaby.
And as I drift, I wonder why
The weeping willows weep,
While summer breezes lullaby
My senses into sleep.

Poet's comment. ZZZZzzzzzz........

John Foster

Aurore

(triolet)

When rosy-fingered dawn alights
Upon my window sill,
The splash of morning pink delights.
When rosy-fingered dawn alights,
It cascades through my darkest nights,
A bright hope to fulfill
When rosy-fingered dawn alights
Upon my window sill.

Poet's comment: The phrase "rosy-fingered dawn" from Homer's *Odyssey*, prompted this effort.

Machree

I crave those massive times at Dooley's pub with me oul doll.
The caic was mighty fine, it was, for slingin' stout and all.

We'd order us two pints o' juice known simply as "black stuff,"
then stand a pint to six bar mates, as five was not enough.

An air rang through the place, a chanty tune they called "Machree,"
that found us croaking blooterdly in gleeful harmony.

The clamor at the dartboard would produce some shocks and blinks;
a local lad would beat his dad, but couldn't pay for drinks!

We'd find a table soon enough, a table just for two.
With any luck at all it, at all, 'twas well nigh to the loo.

Not wantin' to get further fluthered, we'd decide to stop
the quaffin' and the laughin' at who'd buy the final "drop."

Then while the sun was still upon the hill, we'd head outside,
our voices croonin' Irish songs and flush with Irish pride.

We'd wander down the green boreen where clurichauns were seen,
and I'd whisper lovin' phrases to me own dear, sweet colleen.

Poet's comment: A few Irish terms: Machree = my dear; blooterdly =
in a tipsy manner; fluthered = inebriated; boreen = a country road;
clurichaun = figure like a leprechaun.

John Foster

Idahoedown

Hands a-clappin', boots a-thumpin',
Skirts a-flappin', rumps a-bumpin'.
Feel the vibes and hear the noisy
Idaho cowgirls and Boise!

Poet's comment: Yee-haw!

Ya-Du

A Burmese form of poetry consisting of up to 3 stanzas of 5 lines. The first four lines of a stanza have 4 syllables each, but the fifth line can have 5, 7, 9 or 11 syllables. The form uses climbing rhyme, the rhyming required on the fourth, 3rd and 2nd syllables of both the first 3 lines and the last 3 lines.

e.g.:

```
 - - - A
 - - A -
 - A - B
 - - B -
 - B - - - (- - - - - -)
```

As in haiku, a Ya-Du often contains a seasonal reference.

John Foster

Field Day

Locusts in swarm
forming storm cloud
on warm, clear day.
Swirling gray mass
at play? Farmers pray.

Poet's comment: I have always been frightened by man's helpless
awe when confronting the fury of Nature.

Cast Party

Still in character,
I weave into the Banquet Room
recognizing my fellow actors.

"Hey Clyde, still on the bottle?"
she asks, smiling
in character.

On cue, I hiccup, nodding,
and slouch over to the bar
where, like in Act II,
she pours herself
out to me.

But this time,
it's more like
she's pouring herself
into me.

Same dialog, same on-stage smolder,
but now the smile has found
her eyes.
And there is a fragrance ...
(Are we still play-acting?)

I straighten into myself,
dropping the slouch
and my character, wondering
if she'll do the same, and hoping
she won't.

She doesn't.

Sigh.

John Foster

Poet's comment: Having been in community theater much of my life, I am fantasizing about an actor's reluctance to give up his character instantly upon the final curtain.

The Clerihew

An unmetered four-line verse in the style set out by the work of Edmund Clerihew Bentley. The verse consists of rhyming couplets (AA, BB). The first line contains the subject of the poem, usually a person's name. The following lines describe that person in some way. Clerihews are intended to make the reader smile.

John Foster

The poet Ogden Nash
was noted for rhyming mish-mash.
Like him or not, he
could charm the literati.

Poet's comment. My favorite wordsmith.

Than Bauk

Three-line verse of Burmese origin, often witty. Each line contains four syllables and, like the Ya-Du, uses step rhyme as follows:

```
- - - A
- - A -
- A - B
```

The formula may be continued using the last syllable of line 3, line 5 etc. to begin the next descent. Thus:

```
- - - A
- - A -
- A - B
- - B -
- B - C
- - C -
- C - -
```

John Foster

Punch Lines

Bleary with booze;
wonder whose fault.
Why lose it all?
Just a fall-down
drunk, brawling-bound.
Lost in round one.
A sound lesson.

Poet's comment: Temperance.

Matador

Trumpet fanfare, a crystalline *paso doble,*
quiets the roar of a fevered plaza.

Ritual call to worship.

Expectant eyes turn to savor
black muscle
now released into the chute.

Brutish blur of bull.

A gasping senorita crosses herself
as aficionados rise at once in homage
to the breeding.

The corrida has begun
with prayer, parade and pomp.
An afternoon of poetry
and peril.

Amid the practiced dance of picadors and banderilleros,
a lithe movement of gilded brocade, an arch of spine and brow,
a silken agility in his suit of lights.

"El torero" emerges to execute
a bow ... then sweeping passes,
inserting his own breathless choreography.

Fearless swirls of magenta, balletic panache, rising olés
fill the ring as "Maestro" turns the bull,
learns the bull ... and with an anchored veronica,
spurns the bull.

John Foster

Barbed and beaten down at last with muleta'd artistry,
its fury bent and spent,
the once proud animal stands bowed, predestined.

A sword poised, the crowd flash-frozen in a hush ...
the moment violent, vulnerable, merciful, triumphant.

Like any fine poetry,
worthy of an ear.

Poet's comment: Inspired by frequent visits to Madrid's Plaza de Toros when, as an Air Force pilot, I was stationed in Torrejon, Spain.   3rd place for the Matador Award, a contest sponsored by the FSPA.

Acrostic Poetry

Verse in which the first letters of each line, read vertically, spell the title of the poem.

Haiku
(acrostic)

Historically hallowed
Attempts at awareness.
Images invite illumination,
Kindle knowledge.
Ultimately universal.

Poet's comment: In this particular case, I've added an alliterative element to each line.

John Foster

Discovery!
(acrostic poem)

Discovered my poetic muse;
Insightful feelings gave me clues.
Soon rhythmic bells began to chime,
Conducive to a sense of rhyme.
On impulse wrote a contest piece,
Verse for my muse to find release.
Enthusiastic, I composed,
Receiving praise that I supposed
You as the reader might endorse
! with exclamation point, of course!

Poet's comment: The lead-off poem of my first collection, *Discovery! – A Wordcrafter's Journey.*

Valentine
(acrostic)

Vows
Affirm
Love's
Embracing
Nostalgia,
Trigger
Intimate
Nuptial
Endearments.

Poet's comment: A little over the top, but I'm a romantic at
HEART.

John Foster

Blank Verse

Unrhymed poetry written in iambic pentameter.

Encounter
(blank verse)

She strides across the lobby's inlaid floor,
her silvered hair and elegant attire
attracting glances from the hotel staff,
and me – who's nonchalantly sitting there,
the day's newspaper fallen to my lap.

She pauses now to speak to "le concierge,"
then nods and glides directly past my chair;
a drift of perfume lifts my eyes again
to glimpse a slightly wrinkled, ringless hand
address her brow. She stops. I wonder why.

She's older than she looks, I speculate.
A well-dressed patron of the arts, perhaps.
About my age, as well … how interesting!
And unattached, as I can plainly see.

No doubt she's here to book a room or suite,
or bring complaints to management's front desk.
Is that annoyance on her face I see?
Did anger stop her in her tracks before
she would confront the reservationist?

A word announced or was it a request?
I cannot overhear from where I sit,
but see the manager appear at once
and then present her with an envelope,
while taking pains to point me (?) out to her.

She turns directly, heading straight my way
and takes the vacant chair set next to mine.
Her perfume once again takes charge of me,
and so I smile and fantasize anew.

John Foster

The briefest glance at me is all she gives,
then opening the envelope, she spreads
a document upon the table, there,
and with an urgency and yet with care,
She reads and then begins to fill
an application for a chamber maid.

Poet's comment: inspired by a scene in a luxury hotel restaurant.
Second place in Grand Prize Award contest sponsored by the
Indiana State Federation of Poetry Clubs, 2015.

Rondeau

A French verse of 15 lines consisting of three stanzas,
a quintet, a quatrain and a sestet with two rhymes only
in the following scheme: aabba, aabR, aabbaR. Lines
9 and 15 are short and form a refrain consisting of a
phrase taken from line 1. All other lines are of the same
metrical length.

John Foster

In High Regard

Consider this: consider taking pride
In lowly tasks, for when you do decide
To prize their worth, you may well come to know
Esteem of self, the seeds of which will grow;
A benefit that may not be denied.

Respect of others, too, can be implied
As you espouse this ethic as your guide.
A menial job's worth doing well, you know.
Consider this.

One might clean sewers where the rats abide
And rarely see the light of day outside.
Though for this work there seems not much to show,
A lonely life of toil down below
Might truly be considered dignified.
Consider this.

Poet's comment: My father, Willard Foster, preached this credo
all his life.

Car Lot

Crushed flat they lie in rusted gnarls,
their bodies broken down,
disfigured into soundless snarls
and endless wrinkled frown.

Once proud ambassadors of chrome,
hoods polished to a gleam,
with whitewalls feeling right at home –
a car collector's dream.

Now idling forevermore
in midnight rain they rest.
Tears ride their wrinkles to the core ...
at last they're repossessed.

Poet's comment: RIP.

John Foster

Limits?

Callous land developers creep
while the willows helplessly weep.
Progress, with an ignorant shrug,
sweeps its sawdust under the rug.

Poet's comment: Injudicious land development continues as a controversial issue in Florida.

Whitney

A syllabic poem of seven lines with syllable counts of
3 – 4 – 3 – 4 – 3 – 4 – 7. Any theme. Rhyming is
optional.

John Foster

Gutter Language

Raindrops grow
   into trickle,
     starting flow
       into downspout
         to tickle
           slumbering frog.
              Wakes up, hops into shower.

Poet's comment: Playing with shape as well as syllables. Having discovered this form online, I further learned about its inventor, Betty Ann Whitney. It turns out she lives only a short distance from me and is a former president of the Florida State Poets Association. When I sent her this poem, she thanked me and invited me to join the FSPA. I accepted her invitation. This chance connection with Betty Ann Whitney has marked the beginning (at age 75) of my career as a serious poet and led to an enduring friendship with her.

Confessions of a Recipe File

In op'ning up my soul of indexed memories
to eager eyes and hopeful appetites,
I hope someone will find my "lemon gemeries"
and be induced to try these little bites.

The children now long gone, my card's forsaken;
it hides its story in my darkened file ...
Can childhood's sweet nostalgia reawaken,
and resurrect these gems to bring a smile?

In great-grandmother's hand this heirloom came,
its fading ink and ear-worn edges still
reflecting happy times and wide acclaim,
the warmest family craving to fulfill.

Oh, will temptation e'er produce an urge
to search again within in my "treasure chest"
this one thing known to satisfy a splurge,
so easily accessed upon request?

Poet's comment: Looking at such handwritten recipes brings back
sweet memories of my mother (and father, too!).

John Foster

Poetry Reading

As if at a wine tasting,
I inhale and savor the words
offered in silences
adorned by sound.

His voice, a vessel of essential oils,
massages my Muse,
floods neuron pathways,
caressing the ear.

Unconscious mouthing,
as I listen to his words,
coaxes my taste buds into bloom.
Poetic sal(i)vation.

I imbibe the linear lilt
of his delivery,
the sonorous bell
curve of his supple couplets,

and I am intoxicated.

Poet's comment: Inspired by a poetry reading offered by Robert Pinsky, three-time U.S. Poet Laureate.

Ballad

A narrative poetic form in which the core structure is the four-line stanza, or quatrain. The rhyme scheme may be either abab or abcb. Lines 1 and 3 are written in iambic tetrameter (4 beats per line); lines 2 and 4 are composed in iambic trimeter (3 beats per line). Ballads may portray a relationship, tell a story or describe an experience.

John Foster

Echo

Slowstepping sure to dirge of drum,
their reeds a grieving moan,
proud clansman march to richest hum
of bass and treble drone.

With every swell of ruddy cheek,
bereavement bleats a tone
of woeful news, of anguish bleak:
they've lost one of their own.

The Highlands' heathered hills resound
in haunting harmony
'mid mourners aching to the sound—
a daunting elegy.

In regimental file they march,
their chanters at full tilt,
parading 'neath the graveyard's arch
in splendid vest and kilt.

To slowest beat the column plays
in reverential pride ...
The band now turns its solemn gaze
to countryman's graveside.
Sky-soaring hymn, majestic knell
salutes one of the clan.
It echoes still in distant dell,
their tribute to this man.

Poet's comment: First place award in a contest for ballads sponsored by the Florida State Poets Association. This poem also received a "commendable" rating in the Margaret Reid nationwide contest of 2010.

Michael and Walter—Date of Death 7/17/09

Their fame in common, media giants both,
but there the likeness virtually ceased.

The one, so idolized, his fans were loath
to doubt his past, suspected and policed.

The other one beloved, and would beguile
a nation with his trusted broadcast news.

The one, iconic "Music Man" of style,
at fifty, so impossible to lose.

The other, not by any means the same,
a journalistic legend and a sage.

The one, who was "the only one" by name,
left steps imprinted on the world's great stage.

The other's stage was that of world events
which "alter and illuminate our times."

Disparate souls, yet both invoke our sense
of loss with grieving knell of global chimes.

Poet's comment: This tragic coincidence inspired me to
memorialize these two icons at once in the same poem.

John Foster

Sink Holes

In the wake of weighty rain,
land succumbs to tortured strain.

Sandy loam engorged, a sponge,
owes to gravity its plunge

into yawning cavities,
taking houses, roads and trees.

Deep depression settles in,
denting earth's now fragile skin.

Downward heaving rubble slips
into pit's apocalypse.

Gaping hole, a canker sore,
E'er metastasizing more.

Where this beast may next attack
From below, we cannot track.

Don't peer down into those maws
if you've seen the movie, "Jaws!"

Poet's comment: Sink holes are a common occurrence in
Florida. These rhyming couplets were taking me to a rather
horrific denouement, which I refused to consider.   Thus, the
somewhat facetious ending.

Diminished Pentaverse

A five stanza poem in which the first stanza contains
five lines, each with five syllables. The second stanza
has four lines of four syllables each. The third stanza has
three syllables in each of three lines ... and so on, down
to the fifth stanza of one syllable.

John Foster

Food Junkie

"You are what you eat,"
nutritionists say.
So, if that's the case,
I'm a garbage can
with the lid open.

Fast food places
don't have to ask
"Want fries with that?"
They all know me.

Friends suggest
miracle
remedy.

I say
"Oh? I'll

bite.

Poet's comment: One can resist anything ... except temptation.
First place (under the title "Glued to Food") in the Past Presidents Award contest sponsored by the FSPA, 2014.

Haibun

A combination of two poems: a prose poem and haiku. This form was popularized by the 17th century Japanese poet Matsui Bashō. Both the prose poem and haiku communicate with each other in some way, subtly or directly. The prose poem usually describes a scene or moment objectively; the haiku verse casts a reflection on that scene or moment.

John Foster

Fluid Miracle

Casting my eyes out over the pier, I comb the waving sea grass
of a shallow estuary below. Against the slow current of
liquid wind, a languid shadow shifts in mesmerizing motion.

A cresting, as shape meets surface, the ripple then gone.
I crane to follow. A slanting sun sequins the water as if to
dress it for a special occasion. I squint, searching.
A swirl, a curl of gray descends into quietness ...

> sea mother settles
> waiting water is broken
> manatee calving

Poet's comment: Inspired by enjoying manatees and their calves
from a viewing station in Apollo Beach, Florida.

The Course To Stay

He tried to blink the fear away,
to hold his panicked mind at bay,
while fixing now his bayonet
with stinging eyes and hands of clay.

A single stifled sob gave way
to muffled, vain attempts to pray,
the awful madness to forget,
the role that poison gas would play.

The trenches, in a disarray
of death and dying in the fray,
portended horror, grim regret;
a pall above them all held sway.

He had to shout without delay
the dreaded "Charge!" at break of day.
Despite his fear he could not let
his brave men down, not them, betray.

And even now, old comrades say
when thinking of that fateful day:
"He cowered first, with doubt, and yet
no cowardice was on display."

Poet's comment: Attempting something different here by using
the same rhyme scheme in each stanza, along with a steady iam-
bic tetrameter. Second HM in an FSPA contest, 2012.

John Foster

Throwing Stones at a House

Guided missiles, these granite stones,
polished to slide untouched,
but kept on target
by furious pathways swept
along the ice.

Gliding as guard, draw, or takeout,
each missile wears a strategy
of maneuver, its sweepers teaming
to leave the last stone turned
into the "house,"
concentric grail of the sport.

Finesse of turn at release,
skill and point of sweep,
a chess player's acumen,
all play into this ancient drama of
swish and swath—
curling.

Poet's comment: Submitted to a contest for poems with a sports
theme. Fingers crossed!

Ninette

A verse form of nine lines with syllable counts of
1 – 2 – 3 – 4 – 5 – 4 – 3 – 2 – 1. The first and last
words may be the same, or they may be synonyms or
antonyms.

Van Gogh Fields
(ninette)

Fields
wafting
lavender
drench our senses.
Amethyst perfume.
Provence painted
violet.
Van Gogh
fields.

Poet's comment: Remembering "Le Midi," Southern France.

Feeling

She worries her ring finger,
Brailling the haunting imprint
of a circlet
no longer there.
Beyond a skin-deep depression,
the feel of scar tissue.

Wincing back the flow,
she presses at the cruel indented memory
to smooth the tuck,
erase the ache.

Some small success may come
only as the skin draws taut upon
the clenching of her fist.

Poet's comment: The result of a workshop challenge at a conven-
tion of the Florida State Poets Association. Participants were
asked to compose a poem inspired by a close-up focus on a
familiar object. Second place award for poems about an emotion,
sponsored by Poets & Patrons, Inc.

John Foster

Parody Poem

An imitation, often humorous, of a well-known poem, preserving its style (rhyming and meter if applicable) and offering a different "take" on its theme.

Nothing Gold Can Stay By Robert Frost	Rotting Mold Can't Stay By John F(r)oster
Nature's first green is gold; Her hardest hue to hold. Her early leaf's a flower, But only so an hour. Then leaf subsides to leaf. So Eden sank to grief. So dawn goes down to day. Nothing gold can stay.	Nature's cursed green is mold. Her harvest? Death, I'm told. Her early spores can flower. In far less than an hour. Decay beyond belief. Toxic pox. Good grief! So spray those spores today! Rotting mold can't stay.

Poet's comment: With a bit of irreverence, I am winking here at Mr. Frost whom I have always admired.

People Mover

Riding the people mover,
the multi-ethnic guideway
at Newark International,
I muse, "We're all headed
in the same direction,
momentarily.

What if, in our diversity,
our destination were the same?"

Then I spot the UNESCO banner
at the far end of our conveyor,
its doves singing "World Peace."

I think of politics and religion,
the obstacles, the divisive factions:
Communism, Fascism,
Judaism, Mohammedism.

As our mix of travelers moves towards that banner,
another "–ism" occurs to me ...

Tourism.

A force for world peace
and a different kind of ...
people mover.
A path to overcome prejudice,
to forge new bonds of fraternity,
to know one another.

People moving towards understanding.
People moving people.

John Foster

Poet's comment: As an early recipient of an American Field Ser-
vice Scholarship for a homestay experience in France, I came to
appreciate the benefits of international travel and devoted time
during my teaching career to organizing exchange programs be-
tween the students of Emma Willard School and the Lycée Balzac
in Tours, France. This poem represents a plea for understanding
among peoples of the world.

The Limerick

The standard form of the limerick is a stanza of five lines with the first, second and fifth rhyming with one another and having three feet of three syllables each, and the shorter third and fourth lines also rhyming with each other, but having only two feet of three syllables. The defining "foot" of a limerick's meter is usually the anapest (see page 157).

John Foster

To Thee I Thing

An opera singer named Keith,
to Maestro he said "If you pleath,
I'll thing allegretto
that high thee libretto;
just find me my falthetto teeth!"

Poet's comment: Alath!

Bed Bath (and Beyond)
(limerick)

So often the poor bedside urinal
is called to perform tasks nocturinal.
With a dip and a twist,
the target is missed
and I'm witness to wetness inferinal.

Poet's comment: Written in frustration while suffering from a nasty urinary tract infection. Apologies to Ogden Nash.

John Foster

Groaner
(limerick)

A foggy old fogy named Cyrus,
Whose health was far less than desirous,
Cried "It might be the flu,
Though I haven't a clue,
Unless it's the old 'C-Nile' virus!"

Poet's comment: Best read aloud to elicit the pun in the final line.

Misnomer?
(limerick)

A girl known as Pandora Finchum
Preferred to be called "Panny" Finchum.
Once a boyfriend unstrung
Made a slip of the tongue
And addressed her as (oops!) Fanny Pinchum!

Poet's comment: Fanny Pinchum is an actual person. I have, over sixty years, collected strange and wondrous names of real people. When I was a youngster, my father began to file away such remarkable names; I continued his collection and have amassed more than 1400 of them. My first book, *Discovery! A Word-crafter's Journey*, features a dozen limericks, each with a different out-of-the-ordinary name.

John Foster

Therapy Gym

Colorful balloons, beach balls
ribbons and bean bags
seem to decorate a crazy quilt of traffic,
deceptively chaotic to the untrained eye.

A pattern emerges:
one on one.
Patients flexing,
therapists marionetting,
encouraging, charting,
sharing brief triumphs.

Whispered counting is echoed
in earnest grunts, grimaces.
"Just two more ..."
"Yes, you can."
"Good!"

Courage finds its way into the gym
along with frustration, doubt,
trust and hope.

And all the while an easy, light-hearted banter
among staff
seems to pulsate
reassurance.

Poet's comment: Written after back surgery during a long convalescence at Plaza West, a skilled nursing facility near my home in Sun City Center, Florida. The poem still stands, framed, at the entrance of the Therapy Gym.

The Villanelle

The villanelle originated as a French poetic form. It consists of five stanzas of three lines each (tercets) followed by a single stanza of four lines (quatrain), for a total of 19 lines. It is known for its distinctive pattern of rhyme and repetition. The first line of the first stanza serves as the last line of the second and fourth stanzas. The third line of the first stanza serves as the last line of the third and fifth stanzas.

John Foster

Next Of Kin

Oh, how could I forget my twin?
My brother, other self, like me.
We were much more than "next of kin."

As rivals we both fought to win,
yet knew the joys of rivalry.
Oh, how could I forget my twin?

He'd say (and poke me on the chin):
"Hey, you come first, but after me!"
We were much more than "next of kin."

I miss his sly, lopsided grin
and our unique telepathy.
Oh, how could I forget my twin?

His fate to all, a tragic sin,
in spring of youth, how could it be?
I am much more than "next of kin."

I feel him still within my skin,
conjoined forever, he and me.
Oh, how could I forget my twin?
We were much more than "next of kin."

Poet's comment: I don't have a twin brother but have often wondered what the experience would be like. Third HM award in a FSPA contest for formal verse, 2014.

The Pantoum

A Malaysian poetic form (Pantun) introduced to the West in the 19th century by French poet Victor Hugo (hence the French spelling). It is a poem requiring line repetition in a prescribed order, as follows:

Stanza 1
  Line 1
  Line 2
  Line 2
  Line 4

Stanza 2
  Line 5 (repeat of Line 1 in Stanza 1)
  Line 6 (new line)
  Line 7 (repeat of Line 4 in Stanza 1)
  Line 8 (new line)

Stanza 3
  Line 9 (Line 2 of the previous stanza)
  Line 10 (Line 3 of 1st Stanza)
  Line 11 (Line 4 of previous stanza)
  Line 12 (Line 1 of 1st Stanza)

         John Foster

Dragons and Lollipops

Unlike our early childhood dreams
of dragons and of lollipops,
we lose that playfulness, it seems,
when innocence dissolves and stops.

Of dragons and of lollipops
we've sadly grown more skeptical.
When innocence dissolves and stops,
our mind's a dim receptacle.

We've sadly grown more skeptical;
we lose that playfulness, it seems.
Our mind's a dim receptacle,
unlike our early childhood dreams.

Poet's comment: Although there are no metric requirements, I have attempted to create singsong measures of iambic tetrameter. Rhyming is usually abab. Third place award for formal verse, in a contest sponsored by the Indiana State Federation of Poetry Clubs, 2015.

Ghazal

A verse of Persian origin intended as a love poem consisting of at least five couplets. Each couplet must offer a complete thought but need not directly relate to other couplets. A key word or phrase is repeated at the end of both lines of the first couplet and serves to end the second line of each succeeding couplet. The words preceding each key word or phrase, as they occur in the poem, should rhyme. Every line of a Ghazal needs to have the same number of syllables. No metric requirements.

Your Name

In the evening whisper of the trees, I hear your name,
Or within a summer morning breeze, I hear your name.

Can you tell me why, my love, when I might find myself
On farthest slopes of the Pyrenees, I hear your name?

I tremble that a day might pass without the sweet sound,
The sultry sound when, as if to tease, I hear your name.

Deaf and lame, I search in silence for a sign of you.
Yet, in spite of these infirmities, I hear your name.

Heaven's gate issues a call to summon ready souls.
Though my time is near, I am at ease. I hear your name.

Poet's comment: Living in a community of widows and widowers,
I have become more sensitive to feelings of loss.

Florida Riverscape

They glide beneath wisps of moss,
Suwanee gondoliers
astride their stand-up paddleboards,
SUPs to those practiced in
wilderness adventure.

Like a museum's treasures,
the patient river demands
appreciation by an unhurried visitor,
and offers gentle currents
to facilitate the journey.

Long languorous paddles dip into
tea-colored water bearing tannins
leached from trees upriver.

A soft shell turtle keeps pace.

Leafy spires ahead announce
a grove of cypress, guarding
the mouth of a feeder stream.

As if to invite a detour,
ruby ibis sail overhead
arrowing into the backwater.

A wild turkey breaches
groundcover close to shore,
its gobble echoing
against the stillness.

John Foster

Paddle swirls ripple over
shallow moss beds
finger painting the surface
through a mosaic of filtered sunlight.

Heady with wonder,
a young paddler lists momentarily,
captured by the lure
of this primeval diorama

and wonders how he could have been
so seduced last year
by a make-believe
Disney "Jungle Cruise."

Poet's comment: "Supping" with paddleboards has become a
popular pastime for the Florida adventurer.

The Septolet

A 7-line verse with graduated, then declining syllable counts. The arrangement is 1 – 2 – 3 – 4 – 3 – 2 – 1.

John Foster

Septolet

A
proper
septolet
has seven lines,
graded count
up, then
down.

Poet's comment: Versifying the description on the facing page.

Tanka

An ancient Japanese verse of 31 sound units, said to the most popular form of poetry in Japan for at least 1300 years. Style and themes have changed over the years from expressions of passion and heartache and include modern language colloquialisms and even humor. In Japanese, tanka are often written in one straight (vertical) line, but in western cultures, the form is traditionally expressed in five lines often with syllable counts of 5 – 7 – 5 – 7 – 7.

John Foster

Dear Abby

Tell me what to do.
I was married to Alex
for almost three months;

didn't know he drank until
one night he came home sober.

Poet's comment: My versification, using this Japanese form, of an
actual letter to *Dear Abby*.

Cares Of The World

(tanka)

Tell me, citizen,
Why don't you pay attention?
What is it with you?

Your ignorance? Apathy?
I don't know and I don't care.

Poet's comment: Alas!

John Foster

Earthreat
(tanka)

Our water lily,
world's oldest flowering plant.
One strain endangered.

If sustainability
cannot be sustained, what can?

Poet's comment: Tip of the iceberg.

Ode To Grampa

So what if you're crabby,
a little bit flabby,
or take an occasional snooze.

So what if you're gassy
and prone to be sassy,
or yell at some guy on the news.

So what if you're addled,
your mem'ry's skedaddled,
you struggle to get out of bed.

It's no bed of roses;
what everyone knows is
it sure as hell beats being dead!

Poet's comment: First place winner in Poets & Patrons, Inc. annual contest for humorous poetry, 2014.

John Foster

Appreciating The Anapest

Understanding the metrical beat of this line
Should allow us to fully appraise and define
What an anapest foot so poetically penned
Ought to sound like: dit-dit with a DAH at the end.

Poet's comment: Used in my poetry workshops to illustrate this
metric foot.

Betty Selby—A Tribute

Some 90 years ago today, a baby girl was born
At home in Collingdale, PA, one joyous summer morn.

At school she loved to sing and found an a cappella choir.
The way she made her music sound was something to admire.

A sports fan on and off the field, 'twas natural to compete.
Her spirit would not let her yield, nor tolerate defeat.

So many special summers spent upon the Jersey Shore,
To grandma's rooming house she went for fun and games and more.

'Twas there she learned to handle cards—with residents she played
At pinochle, the whole nine yards—a reputation made!

At age 16 she took a job and served up fresh ice cream
And fruit drinks to the boardwalk mob, made money, it would seem.

Oh, yes, up to 10 hours a day, she worked that job to seek
The huge unheard-of take-home pay—a whole ten bucks a week.

Completing school in 'forty-one from Upper Darby High,
She'd studied business and begun a new career to try.

At Del'ware County Hospital, she learned two things with ease:
Vocabulary medical and short hand expertise.

A secretary she became to all the doctors there.
With skills too numerous to name, she gave them "managed care."

The surgeons' office hub and gears, well, that was Betty's thing.
For thirty-five devoted years she made that office ring!

John Foster

Meanwhile her husband Ed she met, guess where she met that
dude-eeo?
They met (You ain't heard nothing yet!) at Arthur Murray's studio!

'Twas Betty's second marriage then in nineteen sixty-one.
She'd borne two sons, devoted men; one Rick, the other, Ron.

With Ed she had another son named Bill—all three are here
To celebrate in love and fun their mother's ninetieth year.

So many gathered here today know Betty for her bridge.
You'll pardon me for what I say to make you blush a smidge.

Your spirit as competitor, in high esteem is held.
One might call you a predator with cards; you have excelled!

Here's to a special lady boasting all of ninety years.
To Betty now we join in toasting—let's all give three cheers!

Poet's comment: Tribute read to a dear friend who was celebrating
her 90th birthday on July 12th, 2013. Written in the less common
iambic heptameter with interior as well as end rhymes.

A Gesture of Words

Gloss Poem

A form based on a single stanza of a famous poem. Each line of
the original stanza brackets four new lines. Meter of original
should be preserved while the interior lines should offer a
consistent rhyme scheme.

John Foster

We ran as if to meet the moon
That slowly danced behind the trees.
The barren boughs without the leaves,
Without the birds, without the breeze.
"Going For Water" — Robert Frost

Without The Birds

We ran as if to meet the moon
And gaily tossed our clothes aside
To skinny dip on evening tide
And ripple water's silver brow.
It pleases me to think just how
We ran: as if to meet the moon

That slowly danced behind the trees
And winked complicitly its light
For us to frolic in the night.
Upon the shore as if in dreams,
We dipped and tripped on moonlit beams
That slowly danced behind the trees.

The barren boughs without the leaves
Allowed a glimpse of owl and hawk
Who, startled, fled our playful talk.
As Nature came into our view,
We stared in wide-eyed wonder through
The barren boughs without the leaves.

Without the birds, without the breeze,
Our special place beside the sea
Would never beckon you and me.
How could a leafless landscape thrive
Or spirit and belief survive
without the birds, without the breeze?

Poet's comment: First place winner of a contest for gloss poetry
sponsored by the Florida State Poetry Association, 2014.

Wind Chimes

On days with windows open to the summer air,
my mother would, with faintest trace of smile,
step out onto our porch,
and then with practiced hand
unclasp the gentle chimes.

A tantalizing tinkle heard
as she stepped back inside the house.

"To hear is to appreciate", she'd always say
while pausing at the S-hook
above our window bay,
curtains wafting in the sun.

And then as if in homage to a masterpiece,
she'd step away with finger to her lips,
inviting us to listen ... and admire.

Cascading prisms,
an iridescent dance along the walls,
in tune and time
with playful grace notes of the chime.

Often to this day,
when I am disenchanted with the world,
I resurrect the memory of
our ritual of the chimes.

And like a rainbow in the rain,
it showers me with hope.

Poet's comment: A free verse version of the sonnet of the same
name on page 42. Third place award in 2012 contest sponsored
by the Florida State Poets Association.

John Foster

Exeunt—A 9/11 Tribute

Emerging dazed and ashen
like stricken miners from a nightmare tunnel,
they lurch into the gray soot of mid-morning.

Coughed up from a cauldron of imminent collapse,
trembling in unison with the ground, they flee the surreal horror.
Zombies choking in a snowstorm.

A blouse torn away, a glimpse of blistered skin.
Bruised lips beseeching a cell phone.

A dark suit staggers, clutching a scorched briefcase,
necktie askew,
like his eyes.

Rage of traffic down
and out.
Unimagined hysteria.

Blur of yellow slickers works against the tide,
putting caution aside for the sake of
humanity.

Heroes are born
and die.

Against a cerulean sky, two symbols of America
have been cleft and left in agony, their wounds
belching fire, spewing terror, rattling death.

Like the mantel of ash below,
a shroud of screams cloaks the streets,
screams not only from ground zero,
but from above.

Above.

Above the street survivors,
above the din of meltdown,
above all of the above,

what remains?

It is an indelible hurt. A violation.
A tragically defining moment
in our nation's history.
A moment to be remembered in sorrow for victims
and in tribute to courage and sacrifice.
A moment to be mourned today
and always.

Poet's comment: This poem has been published by local news-
papers and was read at community events on the 10th and 15th
anniversary of 9/11.

John Foster

Index To Poetry Forms

Endorsements For *A Gesture Of Words*

"*A book like John Foster's* **A Gesture of Words** *is badly needed as a resource for today's diverse community of poets. It informs and inspires us to look at our rich poetic heritage, informing us about the many forms and approaches available to the contemporary poet. It points to the need for more easily accessed information that continues the education of all poets and enables our younger poets to gain a more comprehensive and inspiring overview of the breadth of poetic endeavor.*"

— Joe Cavanaugh
President, Florida State Poets Association 2012 - 2016

"*John Foster, a fine poet, teacher and lover of language, has arranged this book simply and with clear examples that can be tracked by the novice or recovered by the working poet. He offers a palette of forms as both challenge and discipline. The free verse poet may also gain additional strength from Foster's perusal of a broad itinerary of times, tongues and cultures. He uses his material to edify the eye, ear and touch of words and phrases, bringing reinforcement to any "free" home base. For the traveler in this art, specialist or not, knowledge of forms is a good thing, and for many, a vital map of roads for the taking. This book is a place to start.*"

— Al Rocheleau, poet and teacher, author of *On Writing Poetry*

Endorsements For *A Gesture Of Words*

"Finding the right form to express an idea in verse can be a daunting challenge. With this informative volume, students and poets will find a new appreciation of poetry as a literary craft and will be eager to try new forms. John Foster skillfully guides writers through a delightful repository of available options, and he cordially invites them to explore and enjoy!"

— Janet Watson, author of *Eyes Open Listening*; Chair of the FSPA Student Poetry Contest, President, New River Poets.

CPSIA information can be obtained
at www.ICGtesting.com
Printed in the USA
FFOW05n1100210916

9 781513 614960